Running waters
&
Other poems

Malthouse African Poetry

Fatima, Habib and Hajja Alkali, *Secrets of Silence*
Idris Amali,   *Generals without War*
Emevwo Biakolo,   *Strides of the Night*
Emevwo Biakolo,   *Ravages & Solaces*
J. P. Clark,   *A Lot from Paradise*
Gesiere Brisibe-Dorgu,   *Reflections*
Ossie Enekwe,   *Marching to Kilimanjaro*
Harry Garuba,   *Voices from the Fringe*
Taban lo Liyong,   *Homage to Onyame*
Chimalum Nwankwo,   *Voices of Deep Water*
Silas Obadiah,   *Voices of Silence*
Ezenwa Ohaeto,   *Pieces of Madness*
Tanure Ojaide,   *The Endless Song*
Tanure Ojaide,   *Fate of Vultures & Other Poems*
Tanure Ojaide,   *The Daydream of Ants*
Tanure Ojaide,   *In the House of Words*
Tayo Olafioye,   *Arrowheads to my Heart*
Tayo Olafioye,   *A Stroke of Hope*
Niyi Osundare,   *Waiting Laughters*
Abubakar Othman,   *The Palm of Time*

Running waters
&
Other poems

by

Angela Miri

malthouse 𝄞

Malthouse Press Limited

Lagos, Benin, Ibadan, Jos, Oxford, Port-Harcourt, Zaria

Malthouse Press Limited
43 Onitana Street, Off Stadium Hotel Road
Off Western Avenue, Surulere, Lagos
E-mail: malthouse_press@yahoo.com
malthouse_lagos@yahoo.co.uk
Tel: +234 (01) -773 53 44; 613 957; 0802 364 2402

© Angela Miri 2006
First Published 2006
ISBN 978 023 200 1

Distributors:
African Books Collective Ltd
Unit 13, Kings Meadow, Ferry Hinksey Road
Oxford OX2 0DP, United Kingdom
Tel: +44 - (0) 1865 -726686
Fax: +44 - (0) 1865 -793298
Email: abc@africanbookscollective.com
Website: http://www.africanbookscollective.com

Contents

I

"A woman's place" 2
How can you! 3
"I love you" 4
Weep no more 5
We want to love 6
Strangers at the hearth 7
Our world 8
Wrapped gift 9
Famished pilgrim 10
A bride in the kingdom 11
Graces 12
This wilderness 13
Ode to my mother 14
Ma—ma! 16
Kopsammak* 18

II

I am an individual 22
I have freedom 24
Eroding confidence 25
Agonies of childhood 26
Stock-taking 28
Accepting 30
Hurry up 31
Epithalamion 32
Do not quench the spirit 33
To old flames, no more 34
In response 35

I can see through them 37
A celebration of pain 38
Cultural relativity 40
Traveller 43
Death..44
Tribute 45
Death of the mind and body 47
Running waters 48
Nuptial ring 49
The heavens are kind..50
What you think you are 52
The old world dies!..54
Do not stop me! 56
Moonlighting a rendezvous 57
The navel..58
Rebirth..59
I know what it means 60
For women 61

Fortunately for us, creativity in a living society does not completely explain itself to us. To be left in doubt is part of our freedom.

—Duvignaud

Part I

...of streams...

"A woman's place"

Deep down the abyss
Where divergent views are muffled before utterance
Is a woman's place;
A graveyard *sub silentio*.

It is a back seat
Where a majority occupants
In the conference hall
Stifle themselves stiff
Even before unnatural stunted growth.

Alter egos sit in judgement
Over real and imagined faults
Committed in the depth of night
Summoned in absentia
Past jaundiced justice better imagined than told
Because it is a woman's place to be seen, not seen and
heard.
In this part, women should show gratitude
For being seen outside.

Her place is tending sick souls
Made feeble by ignominy.
Her place is scrubbing and sweating profusely at the
fireplace
In show of dedication and care that are lacking.
Her place is the subterfuge steep cliff of domicile
Deliberately made inhabitable to subjugate and relegate.
Both sexes mutually contribute
In modern world affairs
To a nation's quest forward.
Can a woman's place
Currently carved on stone here
Ever witness a reversal?

How can you!

How can you, from this gyrating frame,
Tell how much of it has been twisted,
Bent, reworked and reshaped
To meet another's insatiable quest for beauty?
How can you, from the red, watery eyes,
Tell how much salty water has run
Under life's rail-less bridge?

How does the porcupine intend to retrieve its colourful
quill
Plucked at dawn for yet another's aesthetic quest?
Or the snake, its shed skin
Offered as a sacrifice after divination at dawn,
To determine fast approaching dusk?
How can you foretell divine will from human wish?

Can you distinguish the cock's sweet crow at dawn
From the bird's shrill cries for nest and food?
How can you leave your body to toss and sway
in the direction of the South-East wind,
without reshaping your anointed path
with blazing trails of hope before dusk?

Twilight promises fullness lost at dawn's dusk
Until you can tell blue from red
Two opposing colours of the human mind;
And live green and white --
Blue, green, white, red: all
Colourful medley, symphonies of our lives.
Can the cockroach be innocent in a gathering of fowls?

(20/7/99 at 7:00 a.m.)

"I love you"

"I love you" is
The language of earnest ecstasy,
"I love you is
The notice taken of my toils at dusk,
But "I love you" has become
Labouring in vain.
Had this three-word phrase
Been early and kind,
Had it been not delayed
Till indifferent become
Had it tarried not in hide and seek
Till I am solitarily weak and lame to impart it,
Had recognition sought not in complete rebuff
Till I am known and do not want it,
I could have relished it.
Had "I love you" not been
Another familiar ring in the wind,
I could have jostled the feasting bottles
In celebration of "I love you."

Weep no more

Strengthened by privileged knowledge of who cares,
I will weep no more!
On shoulder, broad, supple, and curved securely
Rest hitherto, vain hope
Which bears such burden
Far from personal but our yoke.
Your creator and you alone
Are able to wipe away
Salty, bitter cheerless tears
From our innocent, babyish faces.
Under many circumstances
Have we learnt lessons
Derivable from intrigues cruel, petty and mean!
Neither weeping nor worrisome anxiety
Can cleanse off the marksman's scar on our body
And I will weep no more
Only because I know who cares.

(20/08/97 at 10:30 a.m.)

We want to love

We want to love
But all we get is bluff and bashing
We want to love
But all we ever hope for reclines and daydreams
We want to love
But all we get is a turnover to the northeast for a reward.
We want to love
But all we get in reciprocity is
The carrot leftover overnight for other wretches
We want to love
But all we get is one, two, three cane strokes
And it is over for the day!
We want to love
But all is emptiness and despair;
Pain excruciating enough to deaden restless nerves.
We want to love
But that again is 'waiting for Godot"
We want to love to eternity
Only to discover we have not yet lived before.
Won't we live and love in eternity
Or leave to eternity without love?

(17/8/97)

Strangers at the hearth

Certainly not strangers
Unfamiliar with domesticity
You have known yourselves for some time now.
But strangely enough,
You're poles apart;
Separated by natural and man-made boundaries —
Linguistically Bantu and Chado-Hamitic;
Severed by a vast expanse of virgin forests
From the Shemankar tributary to the evergreen Goemai
sanctuary.
Complications become complete as actors get
Diametrically opposed in style and aspirations.
Mathematical sense cautions
No two perpendicular lines ever cross ways
No matter the magnitude of manipulations.
Many options exist.
For now, they are strangers at the hearth.

(26/10/97 at 9:15 a.m.)

Our world

Just when we think of them
An enemy in their image emerges.
On the flickering screen
Announcing honest engagements
And just when they think of us
Their apparitions illumine our world.
Their world, our world fused
As a doorless globe to protect
our fragile essence against external aggression.
An intrusion into our world destroys inextricable links
We hold dear to our hearts.
Your world, their world, my world, our world
Are not perpendicular lines drawn on the labyrinths of
our minds;
But fused as one vast limitless matter.
Our world, defying oceanic divide,
Fuses together in unity of purpose --
Our mission of oneness on earth.

Wrapped gift

No amount of clubs raised,
Wielded over our head;
Not even locked, nor closed doors
Can stop smoke slipping through
A thin crack in the brick house.

The gods wrapped a gift for you
None dares open—the power wielded in your heart
To shame the storm raised to harass your roots.

Now someone wants to steal your brains,
To embarrass you for his manhood,
But that will not break your mountain rock.
You have to remain a warrior
To survive assaults of tormentors.
Indeed, "how many stars can rival the moon?"

(11/7/97)

Famished pilgrim

This vacuum
Year-in, year-out
Created midstream
Revived the tasking hours of toil and quest
For the famished pilgrim saved by a miracle.
The atmosphere is tense, yet blissful.
Oh! Leave me not in this eternal woe,
Leave me not in the nightmarish anguish.
Fly these soul-mates into the storm
With a whisper and tender voice
Which penetrates and pierces the heart.
I moan for a dream so pure and deep,
For invisible hands to hold sway invisible things,
Bring forth your watery presence
Such highly captivating, intoxicating dose
To last me for just another full day.

(19/5/2000 at 10:55 a.m.)

A bride in the kingdom

Queen of the Highlands goes
To the kingdom of songs
Oh! What ecstasy, what magic
To be piloted through groves
Of palm trees, bamboos and irokos!
The oil wells dominating the cultivable land;
The bushy fields standing out for recognition.
Oh! The forest, the enigmatic forest beckoning on.
In the kingdom of songs,
Forest serves to provide and protect —
Provider of fruits, game, and herbs.
And the forest protects its own
Against external aggression,
Even as it provides hide-outs for miscreants
Within her bowels.
How markedly different is the rain forest
From the savannah!
The Plateau queen knows too well and loves so much.

Graces

Not all graces are for food.
Once we were granted grace to be our selves.
Even nature colluded with the human cycle
To allow us grace to experience extreme lustre,
A feeling never experienced before.
We are innocent victims of divine grace
With which unrestrained boisterous feelings
Transported between the creeks and the savannah
Gives true meanings to our beings.
Who gives grace knows what right judgement
To mete the just and unjust.
We have been granted grace because
Even the heavens are not in opposition
To the divine mating of sun and earth.

(17/05/2000 at 9: 17 a.m.)

This wilderness

I long to have evanescence
Of your warmly presence.
I feel what you feel,
Fear what you fear.
I am capable of longing as you do;
I taste as you taste;
I thirst as you thirst
I belch as you belch
I groan as you groan
I wail as you wail
I hunger as you hunger.
As you leave, my watery eyes
Gaze into space for a mere glimpse
Of your ever-present picture
Hovering and stretching out
To fortify my longings in vain.
I dream what you dream
I can foretell what you foretold
I am waiting as you waited
Per second, per minute, per hour
Tick-tocking on;
As I long for evanescence
Of your warmly presence;
To feel what you felt, and
Fear what you feared
And longing as you long
To be together again.
I long to have evanescence
Of your warmly presence.

Ode to my mother

Mother! Mother!
Na! Na!
You have won!
Heroine of Mola Dawam Damang
Masterly you trod Lardang landscape, your second
home;
You toiled and tilled its ground from cradle to sunset
That we, your siblings, may live.
You begot Natap, Nasogot, Naleng, Dabong-Damar,
In whose supportive hands you chose to breathe your
last
That we may live
Not only live but also prosper.

Blessed offshoot of Moela Dawam Damang,
We brood over your demise
Forgetting, as with humans,
You are running waters in our veins;
Overflowing, yet constructive,
To preserve the bank
You jealously tended
As shrubs in summer time.

Mama! Mama!
Mother! Mother!
Sometimes I wish you move in that ring
If only to assure you hear and listen
To our struggle through life.
Mama! Mama!
Mother! Mother!
Do I hear your bones rattle in vain hope
Of a response reassuring
You're partly listening?

Na, you taught me
To mother, not only sons
But midwife fathers,

And daughter daughters ahead.
You had been wife, mother,
Auntie, granny, and daughter to a fault.

Mother, you were yet to learn ABC
When you bagged a doctor of philosophy
In the humanities;
Your doting daughters, in learning patience
At the footstool of matrimony
Your only son steeped in agronomy.
How else can we celebrate you, mother,
Than this melody recording the trails
You blazed in our hearts?

Wear those familiar smiles, sweet mother,
And sit agog for a befitting crown!
Mother you have won!

(Friday, 14 April, 2000 on a restless sleepless night at
2:00 a.m.)

Ma—ma!

Ma-ma! Ma-ma! Ma-ma!
I look everywhere but cannot find you.
Ma-ma! Ma-ma! Ma-ma!
Are you at the stone grinding millet and corn
As you had always done before sunrise
To make the morning's pap for us?
Ma-ma! Ma-ma! Ma-ma!
Are you out there in the woodland
Searching for dry firewood
With which to boil our yam and beans?
Ma-ma! Ma-ma! Ma-ma!
Are you gone to the spring stream
To fetch silver-bright water
For use in the crowded kitchen?
Or are you gone to the mountain ridges
To cut grass for the teaming animal mouths—
Sheep, goats, horses, and hens—
That you have to fill like ours?
Baba accumulated these, one after the other,
At divining shrines of the neighbourhood
For your ever open tenderness!
Ma-ma! Ma-ma! Ma-ma!
Have you gone to the nearby farm
To mount the heaps of yam
Seedlings you gathered in season
To try the soil no one in your sixty-eight
And in Kopsamak ever tried?
Or are you clearing weeds as well around
millet seedlings, beans, corn and cocoyams?
The climbing beans and *doetuon* all
Clamour for your single-handed care.

Ma-ma! Ma-ma! Ma-ma!
I search over all these places
In vain hope of your possible presence.
In your place find I silence, dead silence.
Ma-ma! Ma-ma! Ma-ma!

Where have you gone, Na?
Do I go where my ancestors are gathered,
Moulded in a circle, all mounds,
To catch a glimpse of your ever-present smile?
Or is it now a grin I will run away from?
Even then, I will neither see nor hear you again!
In your place, only crickets greet me
With their carefree shrill — they see me
Disturbing their feast on your mound.
Ma-ma! Ma-ma! Ma-ma!
I know you answer in a voiceless fashion.
Ma-ma! Ma-ma! Ma-ma!

Kopsammak*

Kopsammak,
You have not kept the faith.
You promised never to consume
Offspring of other homesteads
Betrothed to you as help-mates
To keep in your bosom
For as long as their union
With your male offspring shall last.
You promised you would not destroy them
In the furnace of your ever-crackling flame.
Rather than consume them,
You would scatter them if and when the union became
sour.
You would not annihilate them;
No, you would not confine them —
No! Not one —
To those familiar rings,
Dug deep, down and deep
The erected tall chunks of stones.
Neatly reconstructed; these edifices
Have housed rich remains
Of those who ate from your hearth.

To a certain extent, you made good a promise.
Daughters of other homesteads
Have come and gone
Like the tides of my veins.

Father's wives you scattered in all directions —
Nalep, Nachi'in, Nasam, Noemulak-Napan, Nape,
Nadien
You made to wander
Like fireflies for refusing
To keep faith with your solitary child.

Two, whose suns have set elsewhere —
Nalep, Noemulak-Napan have

Had your chapter closed
Long before their roll was called
Only a night before mother's.

I knew of only one before now,
Nanaan Nadung-Jongda'an,
My grandma, who lived out her grey life
With Jongda'an Tan, son of Tandang
Noekong her husband, my grandpa;
Until old grandpa himself bade
Fare-thee-well in his dotage.
That is, as it should be;
Old grandma in turn turned her back on us
On Twenty Eight February, Nineteen Eighty Four
On reaching a ripe and round age!
Her passage-on, no doubt painful, we celebrated.
She transformed from being wife to daughter
In order to join Kopsammak's
Forebears in the ancestral realm
She knew too well and had known too long.
She loved, toiled and sweated to serve
Delicacies of chicken, beer, and gruel
Bereft of marital balm in her sojourn.

After that, what happened,
Kopsammak?
You've become so ferocious and cannibalistic
That you devour another's sibling
Graciously given out on trust to you,
A child-wife given out to you
In the year following shortly Nineteen Thirty-One;
Some sixty-eight slippery
Silvery years past.

Na, mama, Nawam Natau
(Shedien) who became Wam-Tau;
Noewam Dadong Jongda'an assumed a new home
And role in Kopsammak.
Mama didn't know, as with all humans,
Her future, her destiny, Kopsammak.

Kopsammak embowelled in Lardang-Goetoeng where I
grew.
Mama now is an ancestor among ancestral spirits
Who people Kopsammak this day.
But this time Mama is
In Loemuat — a home away from home
Resting gracefully amidst
Her step-children gone wearily
Before their roll call.

Kopsammak,
Whom will you not devour?
Mother repeatedly stood in awe,
Her continuous sojourn in your bowels like a hermit
Would eventually, inevitably extinguish her glowing
flame.
I heeded her not, her vision
Instead, persuaded her to look
Not on what you, Kopsammak,
Failed to offer her — love —
But to us her caring seeds
That sprouted from her bosom.

So far, I've seen
Mother was right.
You've consumed her wholesale;
You've rewarded her with death she deserved not,
In spite of widely spreading
Your tree of life,
Your tree, your family tree,
She raised and nurtured from cradle to crest.
Mother kept the faith with you,
But you did not spare her your evil eye.
Loathsome Kopsammak,
You will remain naked in the sun!

(23-06-2000 at 7:55 a.m.)

Part II

...and rivers...

I am an individual

I am an individual, aware of my membership of,
and responsibility to my society.
An awareness which does not automatically
    make me a slave to its institutions.
I am not a mere pawn within a rigid
    and ruthlessly authoritarian society,
Nor a blind, unquestioning slave to the native
institutions,
With neither individual will nor freedom
    of action and expression, and personal responsibility.
Obviously, my society provides ethical
    and social guidance for its members,
Through mores, prohibitions and social sanctions.
I am an individual with freedom
    of action and thought to exercise
Full authority and responsibility as much for
    my action as for my inaction.
Should I then follow my path in spite of parental
    guidance and policing?
I must shoulder fully my responsibility.
Should my society then be so constrictive
    as to frustrate completely
    the expression of my individuality?
Conversely, I am an individual
    but not so individualistic in
    total regards of my interest
    entirely independent of those
    of the community in which I live.
I am an individual, realizing that
    either case would inevitably lead
    to the complete impoverishment of us both.

It is common knowledge
There exists in many societies
    a happy mean, the golden mean
    that imparts strength and unity

in their siblings.
Their essential humanism arises
   from the awareness of an individual destiny
   within a larger, more inclusive communal destiny.
I am an individual within my society,
Whose exploits are expected to
   inspire with courage, daring,
   and mental alertness possible
   only within the context of
   a society that recognizes
   the existence of my individual
   will and freedom of action.
Without this important element,
My society perishes from a lack of
   stimulus and inspiration to overcome
   the ever hostile forces that surround me.
I am an individual acutely sensitive
   and aware of my environment,
   my place in performing services
   of immense social advantage.

I am an individual, not a mere pawn,
   nor a blind unquestioning slave
   to the traditional institutions that knew neither
   pen nor paper.
I am an individual in my society.

I have freedom

There are "no limits
to the assets of freedom."

I want to believe
I can move mountains.
I want to believe
I am free, unbound.

I want to believe
I have freedom
To think straight
  lay plumb
  run perpendicular
  sit erect
  stand vertical
  walk upright

Or act willfully
Without the two chief hindrances
Of apathy and distraction.
With voluptuous energy
And will power,
I can move mountains.

I want to believe
I am free, unbound.
I want to have freedom.

Eroding confidence

What purpose is served
showering the goddess of another
with untold insults?

What benefit is derived
condemning capable hands to the dregs?

And what joys are there
In nastiness cohabiting with gentleness?
Or, how can masculinity un-called for
Triumph in the face of docility?

Indubitably, respect begets respect,
And chauvinism begets chauvinism
Whether male or female.
Womanhood complements manhood,
Both create equilibrium for joy
In little hearts
And love-strewn souls.

Agonies of childhood

Times were, when I felt hurt,
Confused, lonely and insecure.
Thoroughly self-made mentor
To a younger second one
Himself a toddler weaned before sunrise.

Noble dreams, fragmented,
Described, stored and retrieved
As, and when due.
I had a tall dream, tall and leafy
Like the palm tree, grown at
The backyard of our homestead.

An angel wrapped in a cloud
Declared to me:
"Child, out of the toil and sweat
Of your unhappy present
You shall rise like a cloud
Above your lowliness
Soaring to limitless height
In your lifetime."

The voice's entry put paid
To the routine task
Of the sudanic hoe held securely
Between both hands.
I watched the sore-fested legs
That became meat
For the sharp-edged implement of despair,
Labour, pain and suffering.

I listened again in vain hope
To celestial annunciation of yet
Another fragmented dream.
But, rather than listen to hear,
I stared and saw the pattern
Of pain and agony graphically

Designed on my chequered feet
And trunk.
I carry this day, painful symbolic
Patterns along with me wherever I go
A reminder that once I was chained
And now a second time in supposed liberty.

The memory of life in the ridges of slavery
Furnishes the smoking fire within
My innermost being to toil on
Hoping someday I will be truly
Free from agonies of childhood
I sometimes wish that I never lived.

The guardian bird of the will
Once more affirmed
What goodness there was
In store for a struggling gem
Like me amidst stones.
I listened now, instead
Of watching,
For what more needed I to see
Than the eyesore already displayed?

The stranger's voice again
Re-echoed warm encouraging words:
"Child, my child,
God bless you,
I am a lot like you,
Only I do not keep a diary,
And I am grateful to know
There are others like me.
I hope things turn out
Well for you."

In the life of popular poets
As it is, in favour of humble self,
Things actually turned around for good
Only because I accepted myself
The agonies of childhood.

Stock-taking

Marriage is going shopping
In the marketplace
To choose the merchandise
Of your choice for keeps
On face value.

Human goods seemingly admirable
Desirable with time,
Only with time
The beauty with the value too
Of goods unfolds and wanes.

Hitherto, fantabulous, admirable
And coveted turns rubbish heaps
Exploited, depreciated, unappreciated,
And discarded.

Yoke-mate, thoroughly spent
Thinks homeward to pedigree
Homeward journey, soul-mate undertakes
In utter rejection of self
Now reflects. . .

What, mathematically are
The sum total of the shopping
Misadventure carried home?
Who cares may ask;
Not wealth nor looks
For none was stored
And all was spent.
Not even sibling yokes
The treasured treasury —
They remain behind
In the marketplace;
Chained to the patriarchy
That bred them.

Even buying and selling are experiential. . .
Not with cowries nor minted currencies,
But with the heart and mind.
A timeless wealth of experiences
Gathered, are many a woman's
Ageless companions who dared
Shopping in matrimony.

Marriage is going shopping
In the marketplace,
The apotheosis of the trivial —
Ultimate in womanhood!

Accepting

No matter who you are,
No matter what you are —
Whether rich or poor,
Whether insecure or outgoing,
Brilliant or average,
Attractive or plain —
Some people like you.
Others couldn't care less.
Nobody gets accepted
By everyone.
Far more people
Are attracted to you
Only because you accept yourself.
No matter what you are,
No matter who you are,
Whether rich or poor,
Accept yourself.
A fact of love
To ponder upon!

Hurry up

Let me hurry up
And gather modest thoughts
Before they sprout like tall trees unrestricted.
Let me hurry and paint succulent lips
Before they dim and bare the process of utterances.
Let me hurry and gather the rubbles
Before they stifle trial in concentration.
Let me hurry and jot down in a frenzy all I hear
Before they evaporate into vacuous space.
Let me hurry and calm the ailment vaults
Before vomiting vituperations.
Let me hurry and keep vigil
Over lost dreams' seemliness
Before blood-thirsty nuptial overlords
Scuttle creative genius
And confine to solitude and despondency
The ever restless apparition.
But hurry I must to ecstatic stardom
Lest their charitable dispositions change overnight.

I must hurry and scribble humble thoughts
Before they sprout like tall trees unrestricted
And so scuttled, sickened and so surrendered.

Epithalamion

We are so brazenly blind
Right in front of ourselves
Years and years of trifling
Breeds hate and contempt.
Let it be confirmed to us
What we really are—
Though looks and actions
May betray love-lost,
We feign dislike and strip
Ourselves bare of epithalamion.
Nuptial benediction entails
All that is ever done is judge.
O patriarchs of love,
Dole out for one another
The dues of soul-mates
Caught in Cupid's nest;
Attention and obeisance
Yield reunion,
Freshness and delight.

Do not quench the spirit

Do not beg
To be loved
Do not recline passively
In conceited hope of seduction.
Osculate, only on your own terms.
We will reciprocate without second thoughts,
No choice in matters of the heart;
It is flesh and blood,
Not stone; the constitution of our hearts.
Our hearts are large, large enough
To accommodate both friends and foes,
To propagate peace but not adversities.
You are friends, not foes.
Do not quench the spirit
On fire for your facility
In human frailty.

Do not beg
To be loved.
Do not recline passively
In conceited hope of seduction.
Osculate, only on your own terms.
We will reciprocate without second thoughts.
No choice in matters of the heart,
It is flesh and blood;
Not stone, the constitution of our hearts.
Our hearts are large, large enough
To accommodate both friends and foes.
You are friends, not foes.
Do not quench the spirit. . .

To old flames, no more

"To your old flames,"
Barks the raging voice,
"Go back!"
Depicting mixed grill
Feelings of love, hate, envy and fear.
Were it easy to run
To past times' fanfare,
The present would be made more bearable.
And unbearable remembering
Past glories that slipped by —
Good times last only so long
As memories stick on;
Imagination outstretched
Makes impossibilities possible.
But now, is not yet;
Cause unfolding daily
Mounts to rupture the time-bomb
Planted at the hearth
As the die is cast,
A selection vouchsafed
For good to still wither
Accept the woe and prospect
On course
But now, is not yet.
To old flames, no more.
To old flames, no more.

In response

I

Time, not even time can erase
the memory of the love we shared
and all those dreams we two have nurtured.
A decade and four have passed
since I walked the wonder slabs of
Maiduguri's ivory tower graciously built to resist
sand-dunes adorning streets of the arid region.
There made a woman out of "she,"
there earned the rich-filled meal ticket
that sustains her very longings of today.
Today, I wallow in utter wonder
of the memory of loving you.

II

A decade and four when
our love was young and new
we had fun playing tennis
in the company of some friends
your friends, in the neighbourhood
wandering what the future holds
for two entangled in their web
of Pandora's Box.
I wept then and now for joy of knowing you
and thought of somehow losing you.
Now a decade and four are gone for me,
and all I have are memories quaint
of luck, sheer luck of meeting and
knowing someone sweet, and dear as you.

III

Sometimes I let my mind drift
endlessly and in the wind
your gently, smiling face I see

turning to look my way.
I, now am forced to ask
when will I be there for just
a while to catch the glimpse,
the sunshine in your smile
to last me for just another day?

IV

I am glad to learn
sometime, somebody cared to ask
about your loves, your past.
So I learned, you told him
your friends, you celebrate
both on the plateau of your mind,
your big heart.
You immortalize them
your bosom friends
with ink on paper
and tongue on the mind.
Eternal friends they are,
and I, your friend eternal,
you immortalize in songs.

I can see through them

Beneath the royal apparel
The stone faced stares
Questioning looks for undue intrusion
Into treacherous system
Unsure of when comes the intruder
Uncertain of who such could be
Beneath uneasy calm
Beneath supposedly humane postures
Beneath rotund body mass
I can see disgusting putrefaction
Permeating the entire body
Stench-filled and so foul.
The fatty rats feasting themselves full
On what scarsely is theirs —
The faeces-infested body smells!

Fortune only brought them into privileges
They now flaunt as birthrights
The pillage of office inaugurates misconstruction
Of who they really are
Their puffy cheeks resulting from
Untamed avariciousness and "cleptomaniacism"
Of what belongs to us all.

Would the voracious few not stop once
To think that the teeming
Wretches can now see above,
Beneath, beside, frontally too;
Above all, through irritable, craftless,
Treacherous, selfish paths?
I can see through them all.

A celebration of pain

I

Seventeen in unison
Going memory lane;
Celebrate a feast of pain
For a mood pensive
Another hilarious and
Others hearty and joyous.
Yes, we have a celebration
To mark inconsistencies.

II

If only to remind ourselves
Our lives ought to be lived otherwise.
Duration is short
Existence is precious
Vitality is joy
Vivacity is a rose
Sweet and fair
Conditions need not be penurious
If members view themselves
With humanity inherent
In animation itself.

III

Life is honey
If promises made are fulfilled
Burdensome, only
If we want it to be.
It is, what we want it to be.
Life is a double-edged sword
Contingent upon careful handling
Lest it becomes despair
Grief, sadness and suffering.
Do, for now, celebrate a feast

O grief, insecurity, sadness and pain.
Seventeen in unison
Going memory lane,
Celebrate a feast of pain.

Cultural relativity

After the Marxist firebrand,
Only the strong survive.
It is a question of power!
Having set the standard,
The 'civilized' set about
Imposing their culture.
Absolutely!
Cultural relativity, indeed;
the culture of the 'primitive'
never interests the civilized.
Wondering what we are implying here?
Let us illumine;
Let us be explicit
But emphatic.

Culture and cultural relativity,
Our African condition cannot sensibly be addressed
Without a recourse to that particular time in history:
Slavery and colonialism,
Signposts of two glorious moments
of the master Europe;
Yet symbols of gory massacre
Of millions of Africa's children.

Did I hear, "It's a question of relativity?"
Well, Europe prevailed,
and Africa was profaned.
Thus came the dawn of a dilemma.
We, middle-of-the-road men,
Turned fugitives from the ravages
Of our own environment,
We are never the same again!

But long before the meeting
Of 'men of culture,'
The rupture was there.
Rather than speak with one voice

As many had hoped and prayed,
Men of culture discovered and invented
Latent cleavages.
Contact and contrast,
Continuity and cleavage;

Cooperation and conflict,
No real African, nay black culture
Exists any longer.
History has taken care of that too;
The account trails with biting satire;
Give a mirror to the chief
So that he may see his white teeth
Dazzled in the sun;
And sell his sons into slavery.

Give a gun to the chief
So that he may blow his brains.
Give wine, not *akpeteshi,* to the chief
So that he may drink and deal and dance away
While the invader is infiltrating his people,
Impounding his property,
And imposing his power over all the land.

Give a bible to the chief
So that he may hasten off to heaven
Carrying a cross that serves as sword
To severe his bastardized brain from his body
For, he must reach paradise prepared
To take his place as a silent second-class
Citizen in the society of saints!

Is this also a question of cultural relativity?
The paradox is self-serving,
They triumphed,
We are trampled upon —
Europe won,
Africa lost absolutely!

History has made us Africans

The confused clan of the universal community
Even though the theory of cultural relativity
Exquisitely expounded by Einstein and Ngugi wa
Thiongo
Just a handful among a myriad of observers
Tells us correctly that for now, at least,
Reality imposes upon us Africans,
An absolute. . .

And so, return we must
To colonialism naively thought
A milder form of inhumanity,
Which the student of history insists
Has proved insurmountable, or indestructible,
Or irreducible to a matter of relativity!

It is no less true
Slave mentality persists,
Colonial, or neo-colonial;
A poignant proof of the absolute nature
Of Europe's cultural imperialism.
The African, an outsider
In a no-man's land
Lives in double exile
Of borrowed Soul and Society;
Now seeks solace
In the manner of Aime Cesaire
In an Africa of the mind;
Convinced that only through Africa
Can he truly know himself,
And solve the particular problems
Of his new, native land
Undergoing the vagaries of the destiny
Of a house built upon quicksand.
That is the bottom line in cultural relativity!

Traveller

I

I am a traveller
Struggling through an impenetrable forest
Under a midnight thunderstorm,
Faint and gasping,
Seeing nothing of my path
But what is shown me for an instant,
Only for an instant,
By flashes of lightning
which daze as much as illumine.

II

Thus obscured, recognition hindered
And so too the limits of my influence.
Yet existence is wrought with diverse travellers
Who have travelled far and wide
Through divergent roads,
Some, to law suits; anatomy and physiology —
Killing to dissect human and animal bodies;
Some, to tilling the land; the pulpit;
And others, by milking sacred cows
And tapping economic trees.
Yet others, by songs and rhymes.

III

And I, the traveller,
Must examine that road:
"A nest of singing birds"!
And look along some of its windings and gradients
Before attempting a conclusion
To confine myself to the great little island,
Which will ensure continuity
Of human history and civilization,
By the advent of yet another traveller,
Neither a freak nor a usurper
Of human ingenuity.

Death

Are you a sovereign lord
Lord of the universe
Against whose visit no human soul
Is strong enough to resist?

Are you an inorganic matter,
The unknown bottomless deep
With which even aquanauts
   are unfamiliar?

You are a doorless globe
Whose enclave no one dare
Infringe upon!

Your trail is endless
Like a dark tunnel, routes
   of London underground!

You maintain a firmer dominion
Over all your victims
Your cobra takes toll over all
   without exception
No, not one!

When I think of you
I think of you as that moment
When the human brain ceases
To inquire and expand
When existence no longer matters
   to man.

You are stench and filth
To humanity.
You stink!

Tribute

(for Ayo Mamudu)

If only you knew
The hour was near,
For our sake,
You would have hurried
and tidied up the rubble
To pave way for another dawn,

For we are uncertain
Where darkness leads
The minstrel at night
Nor where dusk leads
The sun after twilight.

The motley of thirsty students
Your beneficiaries know
Through strewn path
That you will return
With the dawn
To live the full length of another day.

Even though Establishment
Wreaked havoc of neglect
Bureaucratic bottlenecks
Proved insurmountable
Thus, welcoming the emissary
Of destruction
Heralding the arrival of needless death.
We will forgive them all
With death's seeming power and triumph.

Poet of poets
Doyen of the literary world
That teacher of teachers
Whom the Department of English
University of Jos

Milked, sucked and tapped dry
for twenty three years
But offering nothing but eclipse in return,
You would perhaps have lived on
Elsewhere without these adversities!

Our dear minstrel
Of the Arts
You are the sun
whose blaze confounds
Its targets
Able to return with another dawn
To triumph in our successes
You, who have
By your example
Taught that work itself is
Tantamount to praying to God —
"Laborare est orare."

Death of the mind and body

Talking about death sounds alright,
    death of the human body,
Other bodies, physical and mental,
    act violently upon our body;
The proportion of whose motion and
    rest cannot persist.

Humanity would ask,
Accustomed to death in essentially
    chemical terms; a death, purely
    of animal life: the
    anihilation of the mind,
"What about the death of the mind,
    the soul, the person
    who doesn't just work and breathe,
    and eat and excrete and sleep;
But who also reasons and wonders,
And hopes and fears and believes"?

A high hurdle thus, contrived
In thoroughly representing man as
Just "a part of Nature"
Needs be jumped or crossed.
A bumpless slope running from "him"
    down, through animals and on
    to the inorganic world.

Surely, there exists a difference
Between the parts of the world
With minds and those without.

I, too, belong and live
In the world with minds
And you, to those which do not.
But wait a minute!
Between you without and I with a mind,
Who lives and dies?

Running waters

All running waters
All committed teachers
From the beginning of time
Until now are one!

Just as a spring gushes out
Of the mountainside
And tumbles down the slope
In music and in vigour
So is the selfless teacher
Whose elements remain the same!

Later in its course,
The stream develops and widens;
It may have splashing windings and currents;
It may have broad reaches of quiet strength;
It may be crystal clearness and simplicity;
It may in places degenerate into muddy sloth.

Smoothly flowing gracious river
with all its varieties and vicissitudes
Its basic principles remain the same!

Transparent, even as running
Water should be clear
A called teacher, the unacknowledged
Legislator of our world, our land;
The interpreter of his age, his generation
And of all time remains unchanged!

This toil of mine
A declaration and expression
In answer to a call
An exposition of the tides moving
Like running waters in humanity
In our age, for all time
Can be requited even now,
Right here!

Nuptial ring

The glittering nuptial ring
Is no ordinary ornament:
Heavy as though weighted with magic.
Unlike the wrestling ring,
It's no political arena
For two contesting votes;
Nor four corners providing
Resting place for onlookers
And weary wrestling sportsmen!

The nuptial ring is neither the circle
   of many asleep under the ground
Nor the women's circular spinning
   gyrations at a cultural festival!
It is circular without outlet,
And fortress against undue human
   intrusion.

The unseen guest at nuptial feasts
Omniscient, alone
Knows the entry from the rear
Penetrates to unite couples
Blank, but bound in eternal oneness!

Yet, reserves He,
the unseen guest,
The power, the authority
To resolve, or severe and annul
All nuptial benedictions
His grand design of craftsmanship
Gone wearily ennuyant--
As a settlement for peace!

The nuptial ring proves doubly thus,
A woman's indebtedness
To both God and Man!

The heavens are kind

Waiting patiently
Upon mother earth
Doing my students' bidding
Then suddenly descended
An explosive downpour
Upon corrugated iron roofs
To soothe our dry land.

Now it began to rain—
It pounded down
And flood water rose
As lightning flashed
And thunder boomed.
Though frightening,
Thunderbolt evinces
The Mighty Being is awake!
Greying leaves breathe again,
Shedding fruit-trees
Bursting with life,
Malnourished earth glistening
With smiles of dew
And joy for being refreshed
With new life.

It is no a wonder
Men choose to build houses
By the sea.
For there, living water flows
To soothe frail frames.
How rightly so,
Inhabitants of rusty rocky lands
Rejoiced with the heavens
Over smooth meadows.

"Awake!"
Come a terrifying voice
and hunger-infested;

Thirst-stricken students jolted to a halt,
"Awake!"
Before them in the pounding rain
Stood the heavens blight.

"This is my land!"
The thunder bellowed--
Transcedental power trailing raindrops.
Lightning and thunderbolt bore
Witness to the heavens' kindness--
The heavens are being so kind,
Ever so kind when we need them.

What you think you are

You know the satisfied life
Is the most important hours
Spent with your family, your home,
   your personal self.
You know the benefits gained
   selling your time to others
Are worth more than time itself.

You earn money
So that you can pay others
To do for you those things
Which you haven't the time to do yourself
Because you are busy earning money.

Now you want to have more time,
To experience the many natural
Aspects of true living.
All you have to do is
Set your mind on it.
You set your mind to it,
You let it be your guide—
You go into nature, or
Remove yourself into
A pristine place;
Go into nature where
You can enjoy evenings
Studying stars from the porch
Of your home,
On your own land.

You go where you can see the trees
That provide the lumber for your house.
You stop wondering what's inside
The walls of your house—
You put those walls up yourself!

You go where you can see the crops
That provide the food for your table.
You go to town occasionally for your supplies
You stop wondering about the ingredients
Of a bowl of soup—
You produce the ingredients yourself!

You go where you can follow the stream
That provides your water
You stop worrying about the taste of water
You obtain that water yourself!

You go somewhere,
Go, grow some crops
Raise some chickens and goats
You go where you can wander
For hours and think freely

Go somewhere where
The only thing between
Mother Earth and the Universe is You.
Go where you can enjoy directly
The fruits of your labour.

You owe it to your life
And the life of others to consider
Factors of alternate living
To acting as a cog
In the world of mechanization.

You don't let the intricacies
Of mechanical wonders amaze you
Into accepting them blindly
As substitutes for processes of life
Over which you should have
Direct knowledge and control.
Go and become
What you think you are—
You are what you think you really are!

The old world dies!

The old world dies!
The hues are sobered,
And the quaint glamour of country life lessens,
People no longer tuned to folk minstrelsy
Once cherished by our forebears.

From the early days
When the songs rang out on the lyre
To tell of mythological or ancestral deeds,
Or glorify the prize-winners in contests.
To the days of the bards giving musical
   expression to the sagas of their land,
To the days of itinerant minstrels
   playing beside the great log-fire
   in the centre of communal hearths
   or courtyards,
Right down to the present,
The present is a dolorous period of indecision,
Depression and disillusionment culminating
In this devastatingly illuminating piece.

No longer is communalism
Characteristic of our forefather's world
   cultivated;
No longer is valour,
The talisman marksman of courage,
Rewarded with gold-breasted helmet
As in the days of yore.
Story-telling is now a lost art,
And Grandma can as well perish
If time had not already done so;
Of not being heeded when she called.

The old world dies!
Our lives are caught
In the whirl and rush;
The telephone at our ears,

The motor car at our doors;
The aeroplane on our roofs;
We crowd into a day
Distances and experiences
Which would have sufficed
Our ancestors for a lifetime--
And appalling warfare has
Devastated vast parts of our
Habited and uninhabited globe.

Yet humanity lives on
In spite of all cataclysms
And transformations of the old world --
Our pre-colonial and twentieth century world.
The old world dies
As it thrives among ruins!

Do not stop me!

Do not stop me!
I burn
like the wild harmattan fire,
burning uncontrollably
and destroying everything in its path
to clear the sloth for a carnival!
No amount of water or jet of liquid chemicals
can quench this thirst
in me for self-expression.

I am my life,
full to the brim;
I overflow
and someone there unimpressed
and beguiled of words
Potent enough to smash his spine.

I regale in divine endowments
to fire on, exploring until doomsday.
Do not stop me now,
there is no room
to contain me,
I have let loose in the firmament.
Yet I must give control
and save what is left of my being
lest I empty all and lose all!
But do not stop me!

Moonlighting a rendezvous

You met a gem
A rare gem —
A gentlemanly figure
Tender, warm
Kind and caring
With whom you exchanged pleasantries
Upon a ride offered
At the crossroads of life.
And you were so innocently oblivious
Of other things!

You instantly fell madly in love,
You thought correctly, he too
had fallen madly in love with you!
On your first meeting, perchance,
Eighteen better years behind,
And eternal bliss ahead.
You were dumb-struck,
Discovering the difference between
Many a terrifying wolf in human skin!

On the first rendezvous,
At his feet, the young Cleopatra,
You were stooping
On a formidable route;
Reciprocating sincere honest feelings
You both could scarcely explain.

Nurtured timely by those above,
Your premiere rendezvous
Climaxed the moonlight in your day,
Your day moonlighting a rendezvous.

The navel

This human feature forever
serves as a reminder
to all mankind
to remember that the navel
is evidence that once
man was linked
to a woman's body
drawing nourishment from her.

Woman,
be you forever the source of life;
you bring more than food
to your siblings,
you bring life.
As woman,
it is gratifying to be life;
alive, and the very source of life.

Rebirth

We all need a rebirth
A rebirth of some form
That prepares us a new dawn.
The rigours of life,
The pretense of man
The falsehood of friends
The want and denial of necessities
Call for a rebirth.
A shedding of the foreskin
A cleansing of the soul
A baptism of hope
We all have need for
A newer better life for existence.
But, if the frog says,
The crocodile has only one eye,
Who is the lizard to dispute it?

I know what it means

I know now what it means
To be in want and penury
I know now what it means
To be dependent
I know now what it means
To hope against hope
Without fulfillment
To be guarded
To be wise
To be less extravagant
To spend wisely, love and hate
Not to rely on vain, fruitless promises
To look before leaping
To listen to voices of reason
Not discord, not blackmail
To realize all that glitters is not gold
I know now what it means to curse
To say, "you will see!"

To let sleeping dogs lie
To live from day to day
Pondering on where else to feign.
How to doubly tell siblings
No milk, cornflakes, bread or eggs.
Can they understand and forgive?
But how can they, when
All around them promises jolity?
All within sight are signs of plenitude.
The hour of reckoning has come.
They will be made to understand
I know now what it means
to live a life of dependency.
I know now what life means.

For women

Women warriors of Plateau State,
I will sing your names and honour.
I will hoist your names to the high mast
of the ship returning from your onerous conquest,
ring your names like bells that sound victory.

I will sing your names, women who have made us
proud,
made your gender proud.
and warmed us with your sweet, rare and pleasant
successes.

Women! can I trace back your ancestry that trails
with endless admirable successes?
Can I relive in you memories of your predecessors
individually?

Here we go.
Queen mothers in Ghana were themselves
king-makers and custodians of royal stools.

Queen Amina, our foremother, in Hausa history
military expeditions she led in defence, expansion
and consolidation of great Zazzau.

Ile-Ife's Moremi, for matriotism;
Madam Tinubu of Lagos, frontline pioneer fighter of
British imperialism;
Chief Funmilayo Ransome-Kuti, active educationist,
politician,
up in arms against women's taxation in Egbaland, she
won.

Mrs Margaret Ekpo, with oratory,
commitment to women's liberation movement,
rocked the First Republic's parliamentarians to
submission.

Hajia Gambo Sawaba, pioneer politician in Northern Nigeria
led the women's wing of NEPU.

Chief Laila Dogonyaro former NCWS President,
woman philanthropist and political activist

all names to be written in gold for mobilizing women to achieve
national objectives and inspire with deep commitment.

On the international arena,
prominent roles have your forebears played
in shaping the destiny of men.
In many countries of the world
have your forebears shaken political foundations upon which
the very survival of their respective countries rested.

Listen! Hear! Listen!
Margaret Thatcher,
the "Iron Lady" of British politics
floored all male noise-makers, thus becoming
the first female prime minister in British history.

Margaret Thatcher, in her eleven-year tenure talked tough,
and equally backed tough speeches with tough actions.
Three times her political popularity was tested,
three times she emerged unscathed,
dusted her political garment victoriously.
And in 10 Downing Street she was for eleven years!
Margaret Thatcher is a real woman!

Corazon Aquino of the Philippines
weathered all storms of seven coup attempts.
Corazon Aquino is a real woman!

Nicaragua's Violetta Chimorro
defeated army generals

and their Sandanista's guerrilla army.
Violetta is a real woman!

Mama India's Indira Ghandi,
Pakistan's Benazir Bhutto
each significant roles played
in their respective countries' political history.
These are real women!

In Africa,
for twenty-seven years
Winnie Mandela stood like
the Gibraltar rock behind Nelson Mandela,
her erstwhile husband whose record remains
unprecedented.
A true adherent to the nuptial vow: for better or for
worse.
Winnie waited and won.
What about men?
Men? Did I hear you say men?
They won't wait.
Winnie is a real woman!

Need we remind ourselves
of handicaps that bring down women
across diverse cultures?
If only to remind us that it is not yet UHURU.

Broken long ago is the yoke of poverty
of women's intelligence.
Feeling no restrictions by the drudgery of day-to-day
life,
constraints of family tradition,
the prejudices and priorities of days of yore,
the limitations of social economy--the paucity
of productivity enhancing tools and methods, showing
seriousness
and perspicaciousness at business-decision-making
securing the right environment,
encouragement and worthwhile tête-à-tête.

No longer do you step a good distance behind the men
in your most emancipated world!

O bravely, Hajiya Aisha Mohammed Mana
Mother of mothers,
Mother of love
In form and in ways, a golden dove!
I speak your honour.

Mrs Pauline Tallen,
The indefatigable goal-oriented honourable
commissioner,
determined like a runner
presses on toward her goal,
I speak your honour.

Mrs Uwa Lohor,
the dynamic director-general of commerce and
industries.
A woman of honour and nobility,
in you there is no east or west,
you join the poor at the park and elite at their glittering
tables;
you deserve to be honoured with praise.

The respectable, adorable, lovable Mrs Susan Janfa,
director-general, bureau of information;
you are worthy to be praised.
For at your duty post, you enlighten, inform, sensitize
and mobilize the women folk in the political battlefield.

Mrs Loko Dangin,
the tireless accounting witch of the Plateau State power
house,
sole watch-dog of the state Revenue Commission;
I salute your valor.

Mrs Ruth Gershon Guyit
a distinguished achiever and able Executive Secretary
of the Plateau State Commission for Women—

your duty post,
Plateau women honour your courage to explore, exploit
and explode.

Mrs Theresa Wuya,
the first ever female Registrar and intellectual magnet
of our budding institution, the Barakin Ladi Polytechnic.
Woman of substance, extraordinary courage,
intelligence,
strength, with more than a fine sense of direction and
purpose,
I celebrate you.

Our ageless Auntie,
Mrs Helen Gomwalk,
ebullient woman of international repute,
epitome of courage,
enthusiastic woman of persistence and
perseverance with drive of a runner in the Greek games
your strategic post as national coordinator NCWS
committee
on political awareness takes our women folk
from bedroom advisory role to the nation's
political centre stage.

I salute your achievement!

Our dear Mrs Sarah Ochekpe, tireless emancipator,
I heard your clarion call to women:
"Wake up! come out of your hideouts!" you said to
them,
"your being channels of procreating the human race is
no longer enough."
They heeded you,
and reason germane we converge here today
to celebrate success.
I salute you.

Our budding women councillors,
female members of the defunct National Constitution
Drafting Committee,

fellow chairpersons of the family support programme,
Plateau State
and a host of you other women juggernauts
against social encumbrances have you fought and won.
You all command respect.

The visionary officers of the Plateau state branch of
NCWS,
your thanks-giving is giving and doing.
You give credit where, and to whom credit is due.
You are professors for those learning to give thanks.

Successful, celebrated women of Plateau State
the pendulum of success swings around you all.
With consuming passion, you attained success;
not by sheer luck but through dint of hard work,
stressful hard work, natural intelligence,
humane inter and intra-personal relationships.

I smile upon the sands of time
to see women achieve so much
within so short a time.

A telescopic view
shows your footprints on the sands of time;
all footprints are not alike.

Society is bitter,
you are the salt of friendship;
society is corrupt,
you purify and make it better;
you preserve it from rotting.

You work in silence
not like petrol to cause fire
nor like gas to cause explosion;
you are the proverbial salt of the earth,
you sweeten our nation and make it taste better.

In unison,
we, the women of Plateau state, are saying:
Bravo! Bravo! Bravo!

* NCWS: National Council of Women Societies, a non-governmental organization in Nigeria.